cloverleaf books™

Space Adventures

To Planet Earth!

Gina Bellisario

illustrated by Paula Becker

MILLBROOK PRESS • MINNEAPOLIS

To Paul, my favorite Earthling— G.B.

Text and illustrations copyright © 2017 by Lerner Publishing Group, Inc.

All rights reserved. International copyright secured. No part of this book may be reproduced, stored in a retrieval system, or transmitted in any form or by any means—electronic, mechanical, photocopying, recording, or otherwise—without the prior written permission of Lerner Publishing Group, Inc., except for the inclusion of brief quotations in an acknowledged review.

Millbrook Press
A division of Lerner Publishing Group, Inc.
241 First Avenue North
Minneapolis, MN 55401 USA

For reading levels and more information, look up this title at www.lernerbooks.com.

Main body text set in Slappy Inline 22/28.
Typeface provided by T26.

Library of Congress Cataloging-in-Publication Data

Names: Bellisario, Gina, author. | Becker, Paula, 1958– illustrator.
Title: To planet Earth! / Gina Bellisario ; illustrated by Paula Becker.
Description: Minneapolis : Millbrook Press, [2016] | Series: Cloverleaf Space adventures. | Audience: Ages 5–8. | Audience: K to grade 3. | Includes bibliographical references and index.
Identifiers: LCCN 2016018899 (print) | LCCN 2016023475 (ebook) | ISBN 9781512425352 (lb : alk. paper) | ISBN 9781512430844 (pb : alk. paper) | ISBN 9781512428315 (eb pdf)
Subjects: LCSH: Earth (Planet)—Juvenile literature.
Classification: LCC QB631.4 .B4527 2016 (print) | LCC QB631.4 (ebook) | DDC 525—dc23

LC record available at https://lccn.loc.gov/2016018899

Manufactured in the United States of America
1-41303-23247-9/13/2016

TABLE OF CONTENTS

Chapter One
A Special Planet.....4

Chapter Two
Flying Astronauts.....8

Chapter Three
Cool Earth.....12

Chapter Four
Brainpower.....18

Have A Gravity Race....22

Glossary....23

To Learn More....24

Index....24

Chapter One
A Special Planet

My class is visiting the Space Museum. Dr. Sally, our guide, was an astronaut on the International Space Station.

She holds up a model of Earth. "I orbited this special planet," she says.

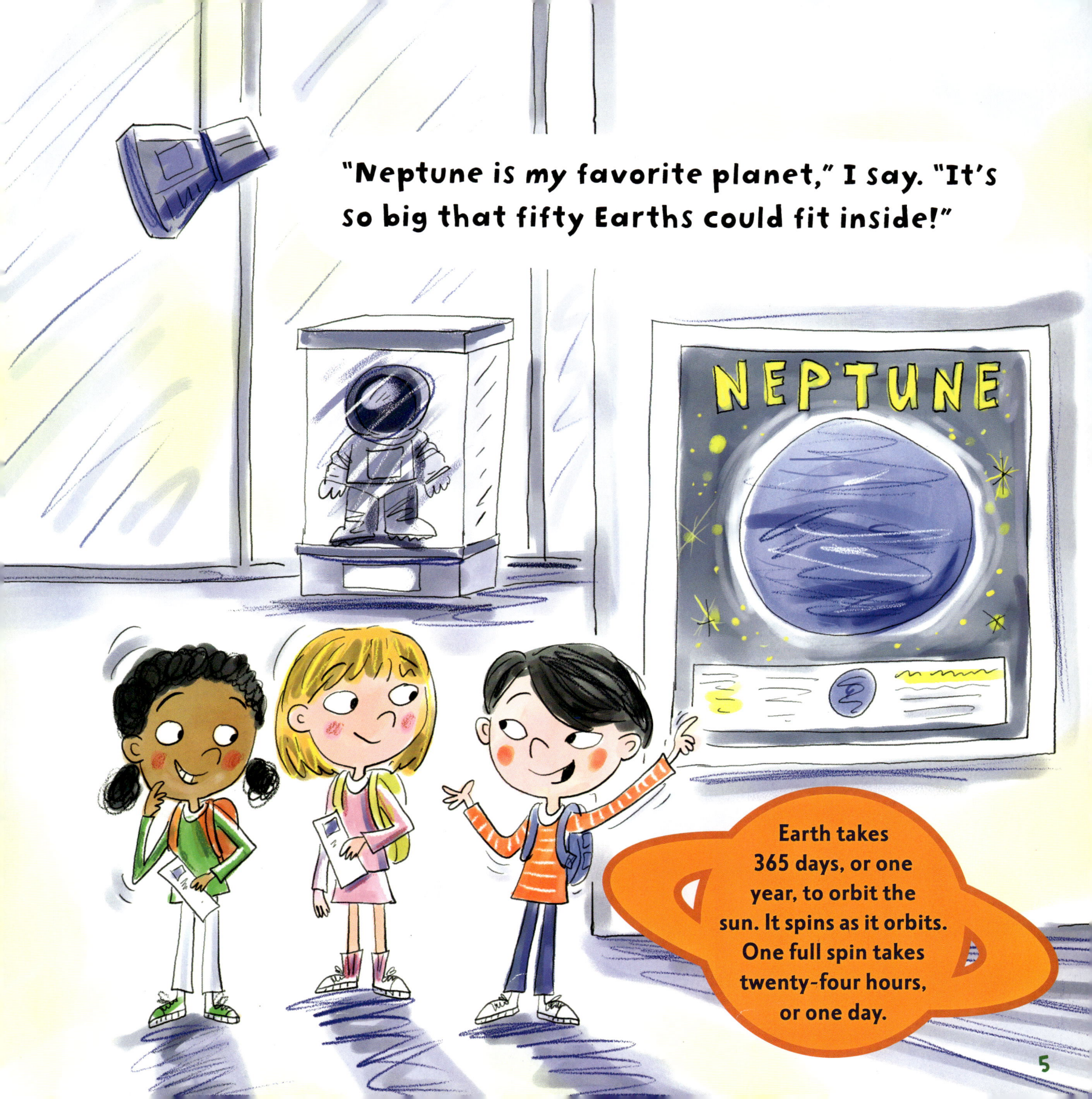

"Neptune is *my* favorite planet," I say. "It's so big that fifty Earths could fit inside!"

Earth takes 365 days, or one year, to orbit the sun. It spins as it orbits. One full spin takes twenty-four hours, or one day.

"Neptune is pretty cool," Dr. Sally agrees. "But Earth is the planet I like best."

"But it isn't as huge as Neptune," I say. "And it doesn't have rings like Saturn. What makes Earth special?"

"It's the only planet we know of that has living things," says Dr. Sally. "Earth is unique in other ways too."

Is my home planet really special? I want to find out for myself. Maybe if I saw it from space, I'd see what Dr. Sally means. But I can't go to space . . . or can I?

Earth is the third planet from the sun. The closest planets to Earth are Venus and Mars.

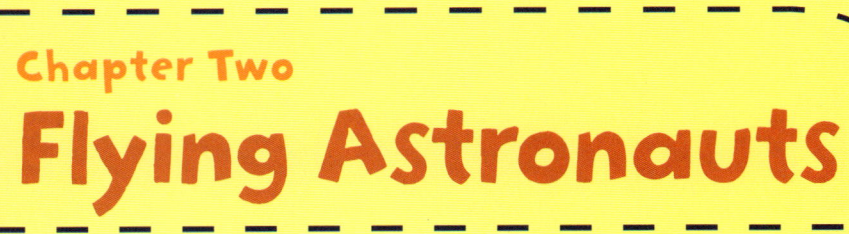

Chapter Two
Flying Astronauts

I close my eyes. Pretty soon, I'm flying, flying . . . off into space! Then, suddenly . . .

"Welcome aboard, Ian!" says Dr. Sally. I'm on the International Space Station!

Inside, I can float. "I'm a flying astronaut!"

Earth is made of three main layers. The outer layer is called the crust. Inside Earth are the mantle and the core.

"Earth's gravity pulls us toward Earth. We can float because we're farther away from Earth up here," Dr. Sally says. "Now, let's check out the view."

I soar to the window and look out. "Earth is bigger than I thought. Bluer too!"

"Oceans cover 70 percent of our planet," Dr. Sally replies. "Most of Earth's plants and animals live in the oceans."

Blue whales rise out of the Atlantic Ocean. They are the world's largest animals. I wonder what other cool animals I'll see!

Gravity from the moon and the sun pulls at Earth. It makes the oceans rise and fall.

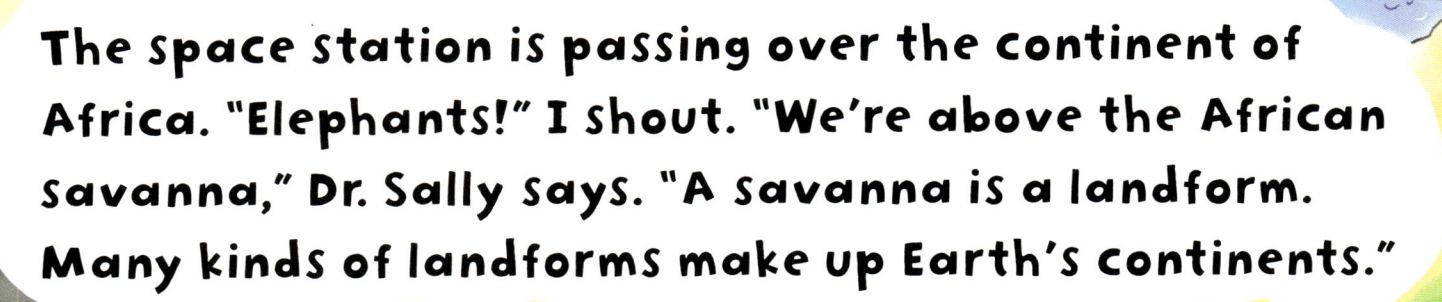

Chapter Three
Cool Earth

The space station is passing over the continent of Africa. "Elephants!" I shout. "We're above the African savanna," Dr. Sally says. "A savanna is a landform. Many kinds of landforms make up Earth's continents."

I see beaches and canyons in North America.
I see volcanoes in Asia.

Earth has seven continents. They are Africa, Antarctica, Asia, Australia, Europe, North America, and South America.

Just when I think our adventure can't get better, I see something even more amazing out the window.

"That's Antarctica," explains Dr. Sally. "Here, you'll find the South Pole. The sun doesn't shine directly on the North Pole or the South Pole, so they're the coldest places on Earth! Pretty cool, huh?"

"Most of Earth isn't too hot or too cold, thanks to our atmosphere," Dr. Sally continues. "The atmosphere works like a blanket and keeps Earth warm. Gases in the atmosphere trap the sun's heat."

There are hot and cold air masses in the atmosphere. When the masses meet, they create storms.

"Dr. Sally," I say, "You're right. Earth really *is* amazing!"

Dr. Sally laughs and says, "Yes, Ian, it's true! But did you know there's one other very important thing that makes Earth special?"

I don't know what it could be. Then Dr. Sally points to me and says, "It's you!"

Chapter Four
Brainpower

"Me?" I'm confused. "How do I make Earth special?"

Scientists are hard at work thinking of ways to protect and care for Earth.

"Earth is the only planet we know of with intelligent life," answers Dr. Sally. "And humans have the brainpower to invent, build, and discover new things. Just imagine what great things *you* will do someday!"

Then I hear my teacher's voice.

"Come on, Ian, time to go! Our Space Museum trip is wrapping up."

I'm sad that my adventure is over. But I have work to do on Earth! My space club meets tonight. I want to learn even more about space. Then I can do great things, like Dr. Sally says!

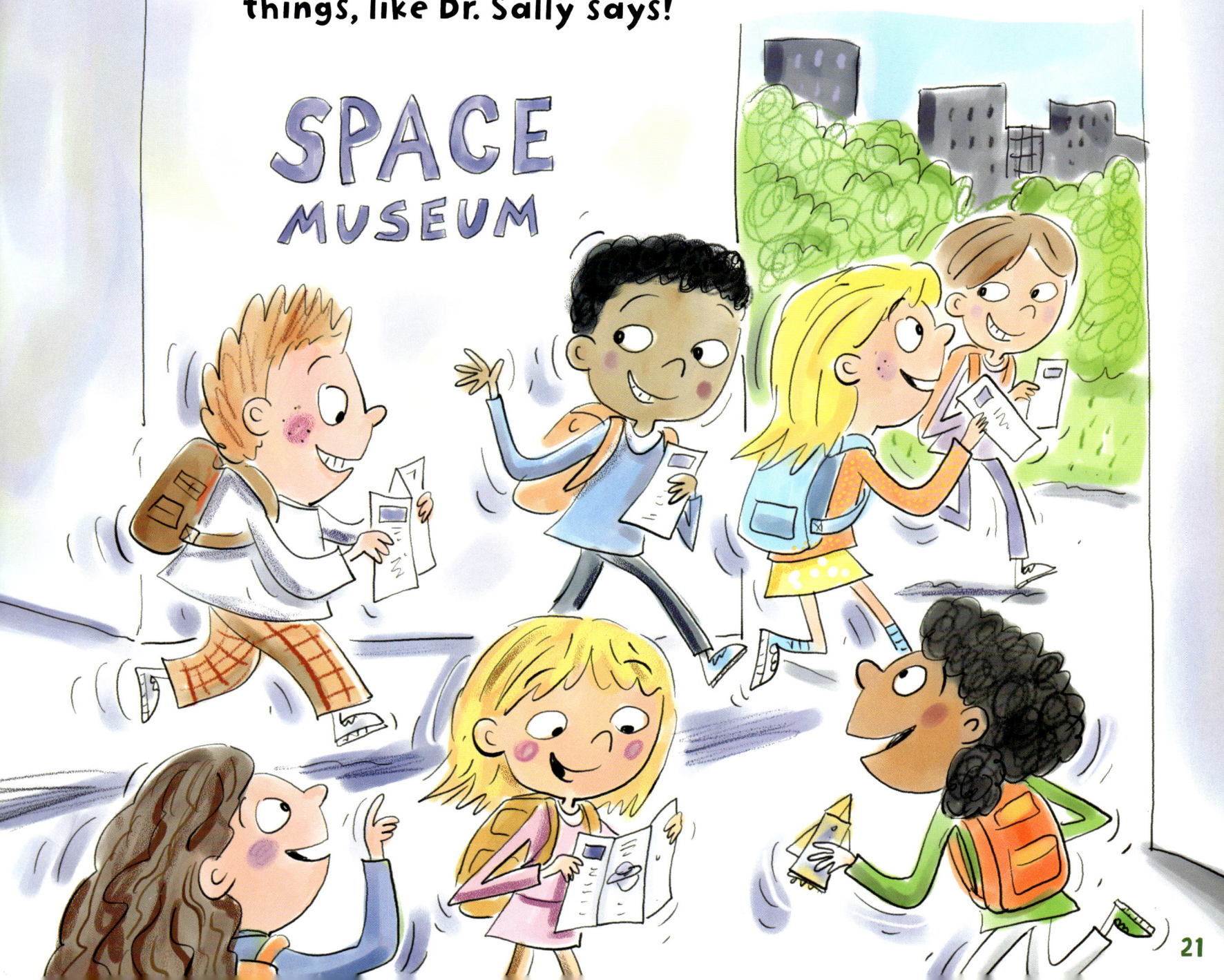

SPACE MUSEUM

Have A Gravity Race

Earth's gravity pulls an object toward Earth. As the object falls, air pushes back on it. This is called air resistance. Air resistance often makes a light object fall slower than a heavy one. But what if there were no air resistance? Would a light or heavy object land first? Have a gravity race and find out!

What You Will Need
a cotton ball
a heavy book

How to Have a Gravity Race

With Air Resistance
Hold the cotton ball in one hand and the book in the other. Make sure they're equal distances from the ground. Count *1, 2, 3,* and then let go! Did the book land first? The book won!

Without Air Resistance
Place the cotton ball on the book. Hold up the book, keeping the cotton ball on top. Count *1, 2, 3,* and then drop them together! Did they land at the same time? Without air resistance, gravity pulls objects at the same speed. It's a tie!

GLOSSARY

atmosphere: the gases that surround a planet

canyon: a deep area of land

continent: a very large area of land

gravity: a force that pulls things toward one another

savanna: a grassy area of land

TO LEARN MORE

BOOKS

Bloom, J. P. *Earth.* Minneapolis: Abdo Kids, 2015.
Read this book and learn why our planet can support life.

Markovics, Joyce. *Earth: No Place Like Home.* New York: Bearport, 2015.
Photos in this book show why there's no planet like Earth.

Shepherd, Jodie. *To the Moon!* Minneapolis: Millbrook Press, 2017.
Kids who love space will love journeying to the moon in this fun story!

WEBSITES

Climate Kids: NASA's Eyes on the Earth
http://climatekids.nasa.gov
This website has lots of facts about our planet's climate, oceans, and animals.

NASA Kids' Club
http://www.nasa.gov/audience/forkids/kidsclub/flash/index.html#.VtcvW5wrLIV
Explore life on Earth—from dinosaurs to ducks!

PBS Kids Go! EekoWorld
http://pbskids.org/eekoworld
Watch videos and find out how you can take care of Earth. Learn what other kids do to help the environment too.

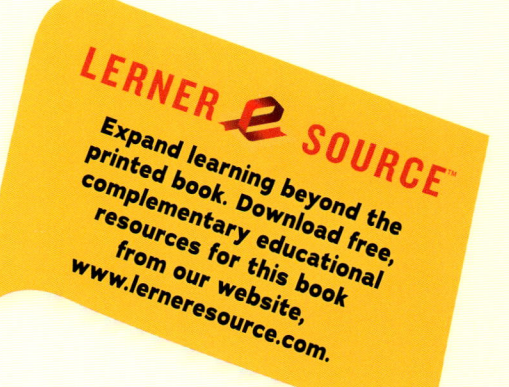

LERNER e SOURCE
Expand learning beyond the printed book. Download free, complementary educational resources for this book from our website, www.lernerresource.com.

INDEX

continents, 12–13

gravity, 9, 11

International Space Station, 4, 8

Neptune, 5–6

oceans, 10–11

Saturn, 6

24